"LET'S TALK ABOUT"

DEATH AND DYING

PETE SANDERS

Gloucester Press
London · New York · Sydney

"What has death got to do with me?"

You may be like most people and think that death is something which you will not have to face for a long time. This may well be true. Even so, it is important that we are aware that all living things will die.

Death is part of the life cycle. There are lots of reasons why people die. Most people die when they get old and their body stops working. Sometimes death can be caused by accidents or illness. You may have had a pet which died of old age. This book will give you a better understanding of some of the feelings people may have about death and dying.

> Although most of us have seen people die on television, death does not necessarily occur in a dramatic way. When it touches us, death can raise all kinds of feelings.

"What is death?"

To understand what death is, you have to know how you can tell that people are alive. When you are alive, you breathe and your heart pumps blood around your body. You can move and respond to what is going on around you. Doctors are also able to measure your brainwaves on machines.

Death is the end of life. When someone dies, the heart does not beat, breathing stops and there are no other signs of life such as brainwaves. To some people this seems very frightening, but others regard death as peaceful or like being in a trance.

> When someone has died it can seem very final. They are no longer there for you, but remembering them is part of understanding death and beginning to accept the loss.

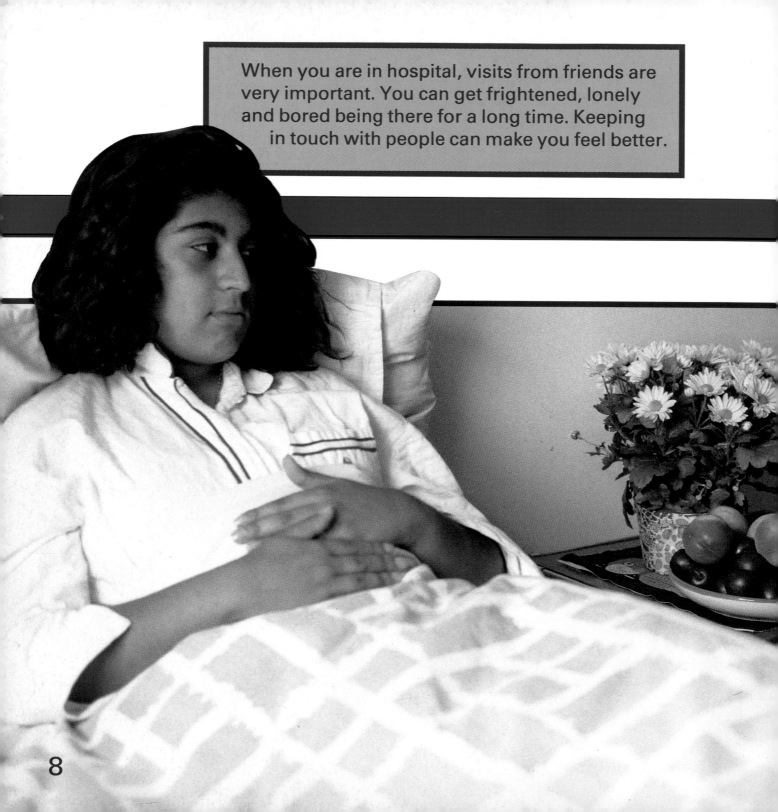

When you are in hospital, visits from friends are very important. You can get frightened, lonely and bored being there for a long time. Keeping in touch with people can make you feel better.

8

"What is dying?"

Most people expect to die when they get very old but some people die earlier. They may have a disease, or may perhaps be seriously hurt in an accident. When someone is dying it sometimes takes a very long time. The dying person may be in hospital or at home. Doctors can often tell if someone is dying although they will not know precisely how long the person will live.

A dying person can be in pain and need a lot of care and support from those around them. People who are dying often feel very anxious about what will happen after they die. They may feel afraid and unable to talk about dying, or sad because they did not get a chance to do all the things they would have liked to have done. When someone knows they are dying, they may feel very angry or upset. They may need to talk to someone who knows how to talk about dying. Others may accept death, and feel at peace with themselves.

9

"Why are people afraid of death?"

When we are having fun, we do not want the enjoyment to stop. In the same way, most people want their own lives and those of the people close to them to go on and on. The idea of everything just coming to an end is a very difficult one to accept. Sometimes this can be frightening to people. We are often scared of things we do not know about. However nowadays there is a lot more information about death.

People also worry about the way in which they might die. Will it be painful? How will I know what to do? When will it happen? They know that death has many causes and we cannot avoid them all.

The idea of dying can be very worrying. Some people try to ignore the whole subject of death. It is as if they feel if they do not talk about it, it will not happen to them. Sometimes the fears we have can seem less threatening if we just try to understand them.

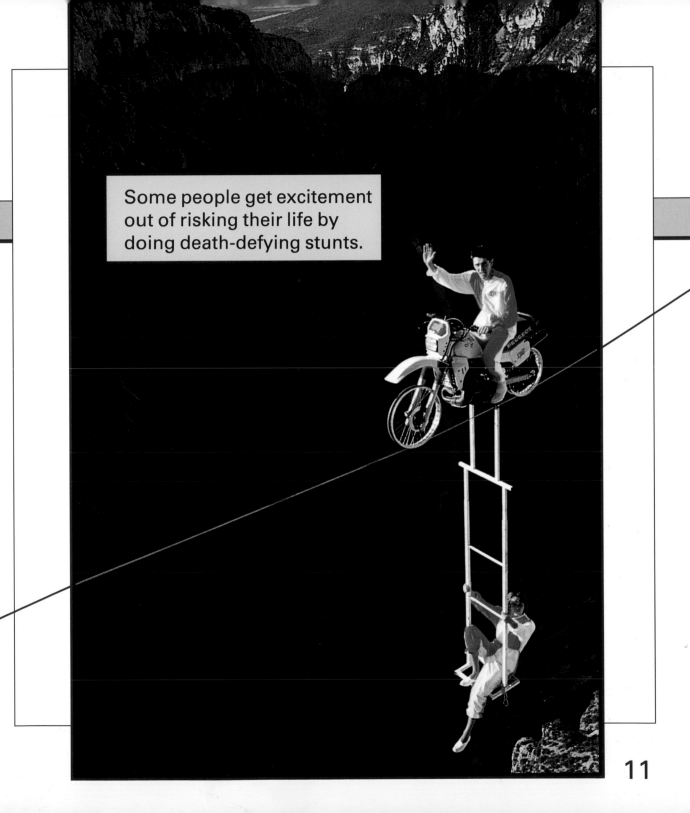

Some people get excitement out of risking their life by doing death-defying stunts.

There are many reasons why the idea of a parent or a friend's death is frightening. Often you can imagine dangers which are not really there.

"Why is it difficult to accept other people's deaths?"

Death is not so much a part of our everyday experience as it used to be. Medical knowledge and technology mean that people live much longer. Far fewer children die in this country than used to be the case over a hundred years ago. In the past many more people died in this country from diseases, accidents, giving birth to children as well as from wars and poverty. They often died in their own homes. Today because people find death so difficult, it is often hidden away in hospitals and not talked about. We even have hospices, which are special hospitals for people who are very ill and about to die.

When someone dies after a long disease, or of old age, it can be easier to accept. Friends and relatives may have been able to say good-bye to the person. However, when someone dies suddenly, the family and friends are not prepared for it. Many things will have been left unsaid.

13

"What happens to you after death?"

You will have heard many different stories about what happens after death. Many people have strong beliefs about this. Some see it as the end of one life and the beginning of another. Some people believe that each person has a soul, which leaves the body and either goes to heaven or to hell. Others are convinced that the soul is reborn in another person or animal. There are those who believe that when the body dies nothing else follows. They think there is no afterlife.

Whatever their beliefs, most would agree that people do live on after their death in the memories of those around them. This may be through a favourite book the person had, or a place they really liked. It might be a memory of a happy time spent together. People who died a long time ago can still influence the lives and thoughts of others.

14

Lots of people gain happiness from remembering people who are very special to them, even when they are dead. Just looking at a photograph of a person can bring back memories of when they were alive. This can bring people very close together.

"What is a funeral for?"

In most countries dead people are taken to a special place. Their bodies are usually buried or burned. Often there is some kind of ceremony. This will be different for different beliefs. You may never have been to a funeral. Some adults feel that children should not be allowed to go. Others think that it is very important that everybody should go to a funeral. They see it as the final good-bye to the person who has died. At a funeral people come together, remember the dead person and are able to express their grief. A funeral helps people to face up to life and support each other.

At funerals people pay their last respects. Funerals are particularly important for those who were unable to say good-bye before the person's death.

It is difficult to know what to say to someone who is very sad. But it is not a good idea to avoid them because you are embarrassed about what to talk to them about.

"How do people feel when someone dies?"

When someone dies, their family, friends and other people close to them experience grief. They can also have a lot of different feelings at the same time. Grief is more than just feeling sad. No two people grieve or react to a death in the same way. In fact people who are grieving may be surprised or confused by all their different reactions. You may feel lost and unsure about what to do.

People have also been known to feel relieved when somebody has died, particularly after a long illness. Others may be in shock, and for a time may not believe that the person has died. They might keep the dead person's room looking the same, or talk about the person as if he or she were still there. Often people might look brave and appear able to cope with their loss. You may think they have accepted the death but they may be just numb and not able to let their real feelings show.

19

Sometimes people may be angry, and this anger could be directed at those around them, which might include children. Others may feel physically ill and be unable to eat or sleep. Some people blame themselves for the death. They will remember things which they wish they had said. Or they may remember things which they did say which were very hurtful. This can lead to a feeling of guilt. Grief can go on for a long time. People who think they are feeling better, may suddenly remember something that changes their mood very quickly and makes them feel sad.

If a child loses a parent, they will feel worried and concerned about who will look after them. Some children search for their lost parent and wonder when he or she will return. They may feel left out and that people do not know how to talk to them. It can be worse for children if they are not allowed to know what is going on. They can often tell when people are hiding their real feelings from them and not telling the truth.

There simply is no right or wrong way of grieving. Some people cry a lot. Others find it difficult to cry at all. However, most people agree that it is a good idea to try to talk about feelings. Grief can be made easier if you have the support of your friends and your family.

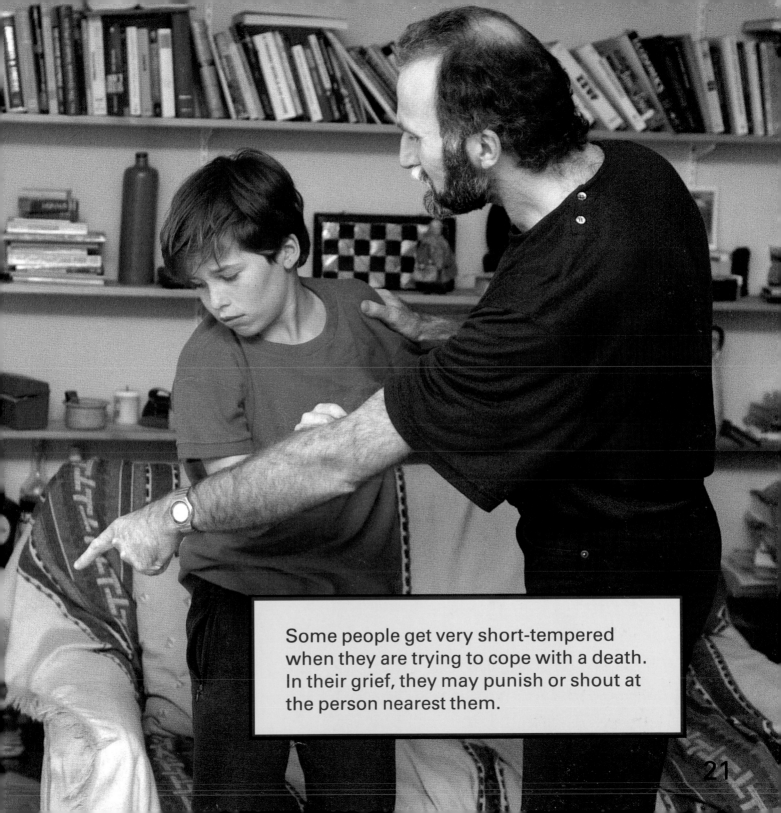

Some people get very short-tempered when they are trying to cope with a death. In their grief, they may punish or shout at the person nearest them.

"How do people cope with grief?"

People who are grieving may do many things to help them cope with their feelings. Often they will spend hours talking about the person who has died. Many find that by remembering the good times, they are showing that the person who has died was very special to them. Often the hardest times for someone who is bereaved can be holidays and special anniversaries. On the other hand, some people may try to get rid of everything that reminds them of the dead person. Others try to replace their loss by looking for new people in their lives.

We live in a world where people like to be seen to be coping well. It seems as if, once the funeral is over, life has to get back to normal quickly. But it is not that simple for people who are grieving. Grief can go on for a very long time. There is nothing wrong with this.

Some people find it embarrassing to express their real feelings. They may find they can only cry on their own. Some adults feel that children should not see them crying.

23

"Do people ever feel better after someone dies?"

People do feel better after someone dies, but it takes time. Support from others can certainly help. Some people say that their religious beliefs have helped them to come to terms with the changes in their life following a death. It seems that those who try to pretend that nothing has happened take longer to feel better. Some people think that they should not enjoy life, because it shows disrespect for the dead person. In time their attitude may change. Most people find positive ways of expressing their feelings about life by making new friends and getting involved in new activities.

> Often if someone important to you has died, it can take a long time to stop feeling sad. Eventually people remember the good things and are grateful for the times they had together.

"Why don't people always tell the truth about death?"

Many people find it hard to put their feelings into words. People often do not know *how* to talk about death, especially with children. It could be that they are causing more pain by not telling the truth. Children can cope with grief better than many adults think they can.

People do not always tell the truth about death, because they do not want to face the reality that death is permanent. They may think they are protecting the children from getting hurt. Perhaps they have forgotten that pain is a part of life and that children need to grieve too.

> Sharing thoughts and feelings with friends can help to make people feel better. This can help you begin to see that you are not alone in your feelings and fears.

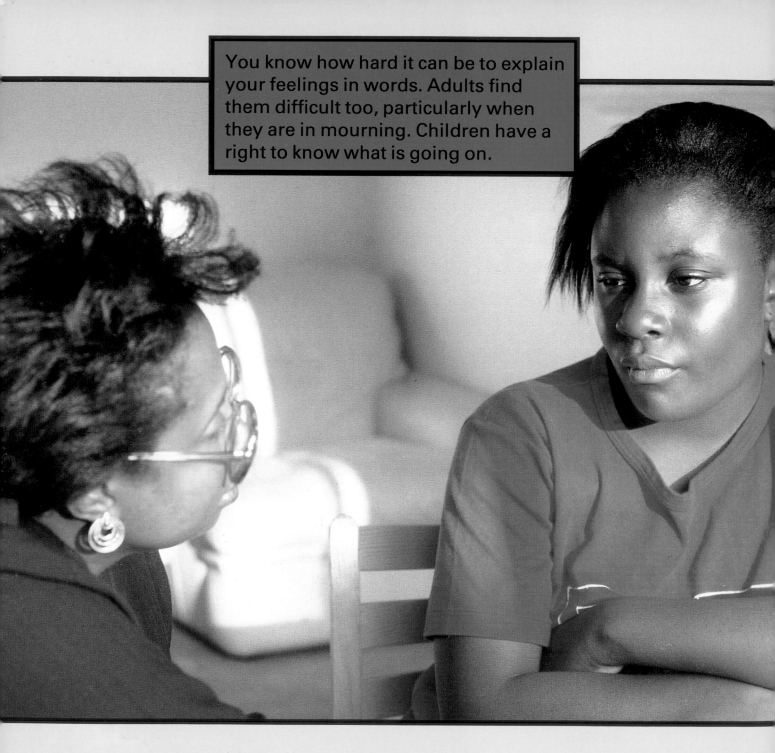

You know how hard it can be to explain your feelings in words. Adults find them difficult too, particularly when they are in mourning. Children have a right to know what is going on.

28

"Why is death so difficult to talk about?"

Death is such a difficult thing to describe that adults can sometimes do it in a way which may not be helpful. Some children have been told that the person who died had "gone to sleep". This has made them frightened of going to sleep themselves. Even saying that someone died because they were sick, has made some children afraid of getting ill. You may have heard people say that a dead person has gone to heaven. This can be hard to understand if you saw the person being buried in the ground.

Some adults do not even try to describe the death. They say that the person has gone away for a very long time. This leaves children thinking that the person might come back one day. It can also make them feel like they have been abandoned. Half-truths like these can make people feel very confused about what is happening and that makes it more difficult for them to cope with their loss.

29

What can I do?

By now you will know that people react in very different ways to the death of someone close to them. Not everyone can say how they are feeling. This is particularly true of men. If you know someone who has died, you will know how important it is to try to express what you feel. This need not always be in words. It might be that you need to hold someone closely. Crying often helps people to get in touch with their feelings.

It is important to remember that children younger than you may not understand that death is permanent. They may ask when the dead person is coming back. You know that telling half-truths can be more upsetting. It can be helpful to show others that you prefer to be treated with honesty.

Addresses for further information

ChildLine
Freepost 1111
London N1 0BR
Tel: 0800 1111

Cruse/Bereavement Care
Cruse House, 126 Sheen Road
Richmond, Surrey TW9 1UR
Tel: 081 940 4818